Juvenile Detention:
A Guard's Perspective

Paul S. McCormick
Kristopher R. Kann

**Edited by Jean Sepulveda
and Pamela A. Pleasants**

Juvenile Detention
A Guard's Perspective
©2016

Juvenile Detention: A Guard's Perspective was originally copyrighted under the title, *Locked Up with America's Children: Coping with Crisis.*

TXu 2-026-371

August 15, 2016

The acronyms and philosophies associated with V.I.P. (Verbal instead of Physical), C.o.P. (Control over Power) and AM/FM (acknowledge, minimize, fix and move on) are the intellectual property of Paul S. McCormick and Kristopher R. Kann.

Cover design and photograph: Nathaniel S. McCormick

Nothing written in this book is intended to replace your policy and procedure. You **must** follow your facility's policies and procedures and should be familiar with the laws of your jurisdiction regarding the legal definition of abuse and the reporting of it, both sexual and physical.

Names of the juveniles have been changed for purposes of confidentiality. All incidents described are based upon our experiences and are factually accurate; although, some liberties have been taken regarding time frames and locations in order to maintain a continuity of expression and thought.

Introduction

Incarceration is necessary. There are people who have proven themselves to be a threat to society and need to be separated from it. What constitutes a threat and what threats warrant incarceration? Those questions are beyond the scope of this book.

Kann and I, as front-line supervisors in a juvenile detention center, have debated with many professionals about how one should best maintain safety and security when tasked with the responsibility for incarcerated juveniles.

They're children vs. *They're criminals.*

Forgiveness vs. *Consequence.*

Nature vs. *Nurture.*

Reality vs. *Ideals.*

We collectively agree that there are no simple answers. Without question, some children need to be detained which is just another word for jailed or imprisoned. We also agree they should all be treated with respect. Forgiveness? That's a personal decision. Are they a product of their environment or were they just born that way? When is it necessary to physically control them? Those debates will continue. Nevertheless, we wrote this book because we felt that all too often the reality of violence was lost amongst the chatter.

Three colleagues contributed their unique perspectives on the challenges faced by guards: Doris Statler (supervisor), Chacha Mahiri (guard) and John Beiler (guard). All of us can appreciate the ideal of a therapeutic environment, but the violence will never be eliminated. However, there are ways to decrease the potential for it. We agree on that. The question became: How does one find a balance between a therapeutic environment and a safe one? Without safety, there can not be therapy.

If you are reading this book as a guard, thank you for your service. Like law enforcement, fire/rescue and adult corrections, being a guard can be a thankless job. If you have never set foot onto a pod of detainees with the responsibility for maintaining order and safety, we encourage you to continue with an open mind.

Academia and reality are often disparate. We hope to bring the two together.

Stay safe,
Kann and McCormick

National Center for Juvenile Justice with funding from the Office of Juvenile Justice and Delinquency Prevention (OJJDP), Office of Justice Programs, U.S. Department of Justice.

In 2015 48,043 juveniles were placed in residential facilities throughout the United States.

In 2015, 152 juvenile offenders were in custody for every 100,000 juveniles in the U.S. population.[1]

Author's note: Incarcerated juveniles represent **a mere .15%** of the juvenile population.

---

[1] Sickmund, M. Sladky, T.J., Kang, W., & Puzzanchera, C. (2017). "Easy Access to the Census of Juveniles in Residential Placement." Available: http://www.ojjdp.gov/ojstatbb/ezacjrp/

Guard:

the act or duty of protecting or defending; to watch over.

(Merriam-Webster Dictionary)

Control: to influence or direct people's behavior or the course of events; regulate. *(Merriam-Webster Dictionary)*.

Power: the ability to act or produce an effect; authority; one that has control or authority; physical might. *(Merriam-Webster Dictionary)*.

C.O.P.: Control over Power; exercise influence (control) and minimize the use of physical might (power) whenever possible.

America's Incarcerated Children

Fundamentally, there are very few components to a crime. There is an offender and a victim. The offender is either found guilty or not guilty. He may or may not be incarcerated.

A thirty-year-old male is put on trial for and found guilty of molesting several nine-year-old boys. He is sentenced to twenty years in prison. In the adult world, that process is fairly simple: Hold the offender accountable for his crimes and punish him.

Now, what if that male offender is thirteen-years-old?

What if the juvenile had himself been offended upon for years by a family member before he was detained for committing a series of violent felonies?

What do you do with a twelve-year-old who shot a ten-year-old during a gang initiation? The Blood Lieutenant, who ordered the *hit*, is twenty-four and provided the methamphetamines and gun to that twelve-year-old before the shooting.

There are times when children committing felonies are merely responding to the adults in their lives.

They are detained for murder, rape and every other crime known to be committed by adults. Detention centers can potentially house an assortment of violent gang members (documented and undocumented), and yet they are frequently called residential facilities or juvenile facilities. In the current environment of political correctness, the use of or any reference to *detention* in the name of a facility is avoided. Call them what you will but juvenile offenders are housed in concrete buildings, a.k.a. jails and prisons. And just like adults, they are detained without the option of leaving until the courts permit their release.

Guards are not typically called guards or even correctional officers anymore. They are referred to as residential supervisors or child youth workers. But, we are guards tasked with maintaining safety, preventing escape and enforcing established rules. We are not walking around a residence; we are patrolling a facility detaining the aforementioned juveniles who have no desire to be locked up.

Those juveniles are also, by natural consequence, separated from their families (mothers, fathers, brothers, sisters, *cousins*) and friends - their support systems. They no longer have daily contact with loved ones which further adds to their disdain for detention.

They have a set schedule of when to get up; eat; go to the gym; use the pod phone which is subject to recording and/or monitoring; shower; and go to bed. No cell phones. No access to social media. They are under the constant direction of guards. Cameras monitor all public activity. While awake. While asleep. 24/7 observation. They are issued generic clothing, soap, shampoo, combs, toilet paper, toothbrushes and toothpaste.

That structure is necessary when guards are tasked with *protecting* and *watching over* potentially violent juveniles. Summer camps and schools have structure and routine. But, unlike those kids in summer camp or school, juveniles in detention represent roughly .15% of the juvenile population in the United States. Their incarceration creates a unique culture of violence and other self-destructive behavior which is far different from the *norm*.

The Stanford Prison Experiment was conducted in August of 1971 and was intended to run for two weeks in order to study the psychology of imprisonment and the psychology of being a guard. Twenty-four adult, middle class volunteers were divided equally into prisoners and guards in a makeshift jail. Although there were, in my opinion, numerous flaws in the methodology, one outcome was clearly obvious: The *guards* quickly abused their authority and the *prisoners* quickly resented being incarcerated and rebelled against the *guards*.[2] For ethical and safety reasons, the experiment had to be shut down after five nights and six days.

During that short period, the adult volunteers demonstrated behavior that had not been typical of their *normal*, pre-experiment behavior: antagonism and aggression.

On 8/22/16, while I was in a restaurant writing this chapter, numerous news stations were announcing the bombing of a Turkish wedding in which fifty-four people were killed. The bombing was being attributed to a fourteen-year-old male. I overheard a fellow patron remark to someone, *How can a kid be so screwed up and kill a*

[2] Konnikova, Maria."The Real Lesson of the Stanford Prison Experiment."The New Yorker.June 12, 2015.
https://www.newyorker.com/science/maria-konnikova/the-real-lesson-of-the-stanford-prison-experiment

crapload of people? Without hesitation and with little consideration for social etiquette, I interjected with, *It's easy: Raise the kid to hate.*

Adults adversely affect children all the time, intentionally and unintentionally. Children are born into cultures or families of violence. Some are simply raised with an overall disregard for the law. As a guard, you will interact with some of them and occasionally struggle with a difficult truth: They are children even if they have killed or raped.

Some of their crimes are difficult to accept. However, at the end of the day, a twelve-year-old is still a child. A seventeen-year-old is still an awkward adolescent trying to evolve into an adult. Even if they have committed heinous crimes, they will act like the children they are. They will whine, cry, make unreasonable demands, pout, punch walls and scream. They will deny responsibility for the simplest of infractions, even when all evidence indicates their guilt. All of that is fairly *normal*, child-like behavior;

however, many incarcerated children will often use or threaten the use of violence.

They are locked up for a reason: They have demonstrated an inability to conform to society's laws and established rules of conduct.

The Human Animal

Our autonomic nervous system is a function of the medulla wherein lie the sympathetic and parasympathetic systems. In conjunction with one another, they control our body's involuntary functions such as breath rate, heart rate and blood pressure. We don't have to *think* about those things because they happen automatically - like our digestion, pupil dilation and arousal.[3] It is the reptilian part of our brain which is located in the brain stem. The medulla is always processing: *Can I kill it? Can it kill me? Can I eat it? Can it eat me? Can I have sex with it?*

When we feel threatened, our sympathetic system increases blood flow to our muscles and skeletal frame. It increases our breathing rate in order to take in more oxygen to fuel our body and brain. Adrenaline is released into our system. We are preparing for one of three things: fight, flight

---

[3] Hockenbury and Hockenbury. (2003)." Psychology Third Edition." New York: Worth Publishers.

or freeze. It is far more complicated than how I have described it, but those are the basic elements.

The medulla remembers threats. It only takes one painful bee sting to become forever wary of other things that can sting or at least look like they can. A hive full of bees will certainly elicit a lot of trepidation and/or regard after you have been stung because you know it potentially contains many painful threats.

A child, who has been physically or sexually abused, may be *easily startled* or respond aggressively to a loud male voice simply because he is reacting out of *instinct*; his medulla is reacting. He may associate that stimulus, the loud male voice, with his past abuse which can be indicative of trauma.[4]

The medulla is wired to keep you alive, to keep you safe. It is primitive - but predictable.

---

[4] Brittain and Hunt. (2004). "Helping in Child Protective Services A Competency-Based Casework Handbook." New York: Oxford University Press.

Once the threat is gone, the parasympathetic system will activate in order to reduce heart rate, blood pressure and breath rate. It will begin the process of returning the body to a pre-threat balance, a homeostasis.

It is unreasonable to expect someone to go from threat/crisis mode to being calm without time and patience.

It's human nature...

Self-Injurious Behavior

Dealing with self-injurious children is exceedingly frustrating and fraught with numerous challenges.

We have worked with some who have sliced open their wrists, forearms and legs. They have shoved feces into their open wounds, shoved broken plastic into their vaginas and, just when we think we have seen it all, someone does something that makes the aforementioned appear rather humdrum. When attempting to maintain a self-injurious child's safety, you'll potentially be exposed to a variety of body fluids and/or excrement. The challenges are immense.

I remember a girl, Jennifer, who approached me with blood pouring from her left wrist. I could see her muscles moving as she flexed and moved her hand. It affected me but not as much as her apparent indifference to the situation. She wasn't *freaking out* or demanding medical attention. She was smiling.

Despite all our best efforts, Jennifer was persistent and often successful with her attempts to harm herself. In this case, all it took for her to slice open her wrist was a broken piece of a comb and less than one minute.

Reality is brutal and unfortunate situations happen.

People injure themselves for a variety of reasons: The pain experienced from head banging, cutting, to genital mutilation may *feel good* because the endorphins released create feelings associated to a narcotic high;[5] they may be intending to kill themselves; or they may be seeking attention through the manipulation of everyone's time.

Regardless, I'm aware of three methods to keep self-injurious children safe: physical (restraints), mechanical (restraint chairs) and chemical restraints (medication). No

---

[5] Hockenbury and Hockenbury. (2003). "Psychology Third Edition." New York: Worth Publishers.

matter the route you go, it's important to follow Jennifer's example: Don't freak out. It's easier said than done. We understand that, but you need to maintain your composure.

After years of dealing with a whole assortment of bloody mayhem, I'm fairly unaffected by injuries and go into autopilot by addressing them without expressing any opinion or condemnation.

You shouldn't begin telling the person why she shouldn't injure herself. If she wants to harm herself, she will despite all your best efforts. Years later, I heard that Jennifer (as an adult), while strapped into a restraint chair, chewed her upper lip off. So, with that image in mind, I wouldn't even begin to broach the subject of why a juvenile's behavior is maladaptive. If you like bashing your head against a brick wall, go ahead.

At the end of the day, I really have no idea what motivates a person to chew her lip off. Not a clue.

Keep the conversation focused on the group and group safety.

I'm here for everyone.

Maintain a calm voice.

Maintain a calm demeanor.

After you have expended a lot of energy, after you have suffered whatever emotional toll you will have inevitably suffered, after that self-injurious child is safe, it's exceedingly important for you to reach out to all the other children. They were also affected: scared, disgusted, angered.

All of you were witness to and experienced something very few people could even begin to imagine.

Give them an opportunity to talk, share and to process. Then, let everyone move on.

Play cards.

Go to the gym.

Perhaps, watch a movie.

It is your job to maintain a safe environment for everyone, not just for the one requiring all your attention.

Then again, when someone is willing to sacrifice body parts to manipulate and control his environment by repeatedly shoving feces, chicken bones and Monopoly™ pieces into his arm (after ripping out the stitches received during a surgery to save his arm from an infection), what the hell do you do?

AM / FM

Acknowledge the injury.
Minimize talking about it.
Fix the injury.
Move on.

It may seem callous, but it's sage advice. A self-injurious juvenile can suck the life out of all the guards and all the other juveniles in a facility. The continual exposure to blood and the continual need to keep the juvenile safe from himself is physically and psychologically exhausting. That juvenile, who you are protecting from himself, is the same one who has bitten you, headbutted you, punched you and thrown piss on you. There's a fine line between indifference and being pragmatic in your approach. Indifference, at the minimum, will get you suspended or, the worst-case scenario, may result in the death of the juvenile or termination. Be pragmatic.

AM/FM

From Orphanage to Detention

John Beiler

My journey with children in crisis began in late 2010 when I packed up what I had of my life in the United States and moved to the beautiful rugged country of Mexico for four years to work with boys who had survived severe emotional and physical trauma. Living in an orphanage with some of the most underprivileged children in today's society has inevitably left its stamp on my life. I became a father figure they never had. I listened to their stories: crying with them, laughing. I read them bedtime stories and played games with them. I helped with their homework. I'd wash their laundry and buy them Christmas gifts. In many ways, those relationships are the closest ties I've ever had to break, apart from my own family.

Now, instead of a hard-packed desert terrain and dancing mountain peaks, I find myself surrounded by cold concrete walls, walking over the even colder concrete floors. Heavy cell doors, that ring with a note of dread every time they open or close, outline the perimeters of day rooms and cells.

Violence in this profession is inevitable. I get it. In that orphanage, I was exposed to violence like I had never seen before. I could share story upon story of having been spit on, bitten or of restraining kids in an attempt to keep them and those around them safe. Now, in detention, I'm face-to-face with a reality that every time I walk through these doors, I may become a victim of violence. More times than not, I wish I could turn around and go back home. There's a *jailhouse* brutality that far exceeds any of my previous experiences.

I've seen way too many people get seriously hurt, kids and staff. While I wish there was an answer, I don't believe there is one. Being surrounded by kids who have known nothing but this way of life, totally eradicating violence is not going to happen.

A detention center is obviously not the ideal place for any child to live, much like an orphanage isn't the perfect place for a child to be raised. But sometimes, those are the best options.

So, whether in an Mexican orphanage or an U.S. detention facility: Treat children, under your care, with respect no matter their past circumstances. Even if they have attacked you, you must summon the strength to treat them respectfully. Always make it a priority to provide a safe environment: create emotional safety for a child who has entrusted his story to you and provide physical safety for yourself, coworkers and the other children.

Complacency and Friends

Incarcerated juveniles spend their days watching you and figuring out your weaknesses. If you consistently become upset at being called fat, especially if you are and sensitive to it, you'll most likely fail in this career. They'll enjoy targeting you (day in and day out).

You have to calmly address issues as they happen.

Recently, fourteen hours into my second consecutive sixteen-hour shift and after a restraint during which I further tweaked my already aching back, a detainee, David (seventeen-years-old, knocking at eighteen), asked me why I did what I did? I told him, *I actually give a shit about you guys.* He responded, *That's cool, someone has to.*

He was a rough character, incarcerated for assault by mob (gang related) and brandishing a firearm; but he had his likeable moments, and we could reason with each other.

Unlike many jobs that allow you continual interaction with other adults and the opportunity for non-work-related conversation, you'll essentially be incarcerated for an entire shift.

When you walk into your facility, any and all personal problems must be left at the door. You have to be one-hundred percent focused. It doesn't matter if you're having relationship problems, a family member is dying or you're experiencing financial difficulty and wondering how you'll pay the past due rent. You have to let it go. If not, you'll be distracted and increase the odds of being hurt because you didn't see the assault coming at you, or you will miss the possible indicators that an assault on another child is imminent.

You can't unburden your personal problems on an apparently *caring* and *compassionate* juvenile. He has his own myriad of issues and shouldn't be made to feel responsible for or given control over your emotional state. The other detainees will notice your favoritism and the rumors will inevitably begin which will precipitate that downward spiral into regret and consequence. Never believe that an incarcerated child is your friend.

I will never trust a detainee again.

One could rightfully infer from that statement a belief that *They're all out to get me*, but that's not my implication. If you allow yourself to trust one juvenile, you'll let your *defenses down* with him. He may never be a threat to you, but (if you have let them down) it increases the odds of you letting your defenses down with another and so on and so forth. Before you know it, you will have become complacent, and complacency will get you and other people hurt.

In the mid-1990s, I walked onto a secure psychiatric unit to start my shift as a residential aide and saw Johnnie approaching. I kind of *trusted* him. He'd been on the unit for a couple of months and had assaulted many aides but not me. I should have noticed that he was walking quickly with clenched fists. I should have noticed that he wasn't smiling. In retrospect, he looked pissed off; but I missed all that. After all, it was Johnnie. Before I could ask, *What's going on?* he punched me in the face. It took numerous staff to pull him off. He gave me a good black eye and a fat lip to go with it.

I finished my shift sore and humiliated. Johnnie had beaten my ass because the previous day I had forgotten to get him a pen.

Although I can be friendly with the children, I am not their friend. There's an important and distinct difference. Being friendly is about overt behavior toward someone: non-threatening, engaging, pleasant and non-judgmental. Being friends is about an emotional connection: a common bond due to interests, a sharing of intimate and personal information.

You will be spending your days surrounded by people who aren't your friends. Like in any adult jail or prison, the incarcerated individuals outnumber the guards. When push comes to shove, they are not your friends.

Not long ago, we were involved in a riot in the gym. More children were attacking each other and the guards than we had available guards in the facility. I watched a guard being choked while he was restraining another kid. I was helpless to do anything because I could not release my combatant. If I had, he would have resumed rioting; he was determined and taking every bit of strength I had to maintain control.

The whole situation was contained within minutes, but it will always serve as a reminder that the potential for chaos (multiple occurring crises) is always lurking.[6]

---

[6] The riot occurred because earlier in the shift one detainee had disrespected another detainee's home country. Factions formed. Battle lines were drawn.

There wasn't time for us to debrief. Once the rioters were safely secured in their respective rooms, we were tasked with resuming our work with the other juveniles with needs and demands.

Many of them were angry because they had to be locked down so their guards could respond to the riot.

It's not fair! This is bullshit! Fuck you!

Tapping Out

The first time I heard the term *tapping out* was in reference to a restraint. A restraint is a fight. Fights are exhausting.

Tapping out can also refer to when a resident just isn't responding to your verbal redirection. Maybe, another voice is all it will take to get him to do whatever it is he needs to do.

They have all day, every day, to pick up on your habits. They'll talk about you and how you interact with them and the other guards. They'll find your triggers - what irritates the hell out of you. There is no shame in admitting that you have been taken to a breaking point. People get on each other's nerves. It's better to call for assistance and excuse yourself from a situation before you say or do something you and the detainee may regret.

Be willing to acknowledge when you are no longer being therapeutic.

Be willing to tap out.

Coping with Crisis

Whenever possible be VIP: **V**erbal **I**nstead of **P**hysical.

However, no matter how hard you try, there will be violence. Regardless of any rapport you may have with a juvenile, despite doing and saying everything correctly, it will occur.

We asked a few juveniles for their thoughts on seeing one of their peers restrained. There was a common response: Although they agreed most physical interventions were necessary to keep everyone safe, they did feel some staff would try to hurt them during the process.

We had been clear that we didn't want them to mention names but when certain characteristics, both verbal and physical, were described, we could reasonably identify the guards, including ourselves.

We all have certain mannerisms that make us unique: how we talk, move and our facial expressions. Some of us are more aggressive than others. Others are more defensive. Extrovert. Introvert. The guards perceived as being overly aggressive and intending harm had often expressed a belief that it was the job of the facility to punish the juveniles for their various transgressions. It's the guard's *job to set them straight* and *let them know who's boss.*

We're not saying the staff seemingly described were or are abusive. Not at all. However, there's a reasonable correlation to be made: If you feel someone is deserving of punishment, you are more likely to interact with him aggressively (when he's in crisis) which can potentially escalate an already volatile situation into something even more dangerous.

Your attitude toward a person can affect how you physically manage him when he's in crisis. A judgmental attitude will negatively affect behavior, yours and the theirs.

Many of our so-called-juveniles can be a lot bigger and stronger than us. Some will punch, kick and throw heavy meal trays at us; plastic chairs may be smashed over our heads; but, by assuming the responsibilities of a guard, we have assumed the risks and are trained to do no harm. That has to be our prevailing attitude: Do no harm.

Not long ago, a fellow guard was involved with separating two combative juveniles. He had successfully restrained one on the floor while a second guard was attempting to restrain the other kid. The guard on the ground purposefully rolled his body so that his back took the brunt of the kicks intended for the juvenile under his power and control until the other guard fully restrained his juvenile.

Many guards have done something similar. We are expected to.

During those moments you need to be aware of what you're saying, how you're saying it and the volume of your voice. Verbal techniques don't cease to exist because you have applied a physical restraint. You can be executing one perfectly but be perceived as aggressive or physically abusive because of your voice and the words you chose to use.

Perception is reality.

If you're yelling commands at someone, he's more likely to react than to listen. Yelling at someone to calm down (while you're restraining him) is unlikely to achieve the desired response. You'll have more success if you say, *It'll be okay*; something other than, *Calm the hell down!*

It's easy to lose control of your voice. You're in a fight. You're jacked up. We understand. We've been there.

Once you put hands on someone, you have started the process of taking all power and control from him and (for him) it's scary. On a very primitive level, he's having his survival threatened. At that moment, you may as well be a grizzly bear.

He may be yelling, screaming and/or demanding his immediate release.

Why the fuck are you hurting me?
Get off me asshole!
I'll kill you!
Fuck you and your mother!

Don't respond to anything remotely similar to those aforementioned tirades. Keep reassuring him (and yourself) that you are there to keep him safe. Don't acknowledge his words because they are just that, words. More often than not, silence is best because rarely is anything positive elicited from a battle of ill-conceived words. He has lost power and can only hope to regain control by evoking an emotional response from you.

You need to be patient and take controlled breaths.

Don't laugh at the vitriol because you could be perceived as dismissive which will most likely cause further escalation. Years ago, a guard laughed when a detainee threatened to *shove a dildo up* the guard's ass and make him his *bitch*. When the guard laughed, the kid became more enraged and successfully punched him.

It comes with experience. Having been involved with hundreds of crises, I am much calmer in my approach now than I was during my first several dozen. I talk and listen a lot more. If I can help someone *save face* by giving him a series of options of which mine is really the only one, I will.

Hey, let's go to your room. We'll talk there. I'll hear you out. Let's go, now.

VIP

What Did You Say?

Some kids just can't be helped at the time you're trying to help them. They like how they are living. Detention is part of what they know.

I asked a resident what he wanted when he got out? He said he couldn't wait to turn eighteen because after he was arrested he would go to jail and, at least, see his dad. Again, it's what he knows.

I couldn't have done this job when I was twenty-years-old because of the crap talk, that incessant bullshit of: *I fucked your mom*; *Your wife wants my dick*; and *Your mom's a bitch*.

My favorite utterance was, *I swear I'm gonna fuck your mom on my mom*. I'm still not one-hundred percent sure what he meant by that, but none of it should become personal. They don't know your wife or mother. They just want to get you flustered, off your game.

It's all too easy for detainees to gain control through words. You can't win an argument with a pissed off kid. There's absolutely nothing to be gained by verbally engaging him. Nothing.

Not long ago, a guard, someone I fully respected, had become overly worked up. He was pissed off and reacting to a kid who was verbally attacking him from behind a secured steel door: cursing at him; calling him names; telling him how he would *rape* his pregnant wife.

The guard responded loudly, *I'm not scared of you*, and opened the kid's door and continued with, *What are you going to do?* Then yelled, *I don't see you talking now.*

I sent the guard away, tapped him out. I had to. All the while, the juvenile had come out of his room, refusing to return. He was verbally antagonizing us.

Assuming there was nothing to lose, I walked over to him and asked, *Would you please go back into your room?* He looked at me and said, *OK, but only because you said,* ***"Please"***.

To me he was being a *smart ass*, but he did go into his room. I locked him down.

Power is making someone do what you want them to do. Control is guiding them to do what you want, when you want, without force.

Many guards will have the power to make most residents do what they want, by physical force. Not every guard will have the ability to control the situation through words. A balance of the two is ideal.

I have great difficulty being patient with entitled children. They wear me down faster than damn near anything else. Their constant demands for instant responses to their requests, regardless of whatever else may be going on, test my patience more than highly aggressive children. I can feel my blood pressure instantly increase when I hear their voices as I enter a pod.

There was one child in particular who, when I heard was returning to our facility, made me consider, albeit briefly, another career. He wasn't violent or self-injurious. For the most part, he was polite and respectful, but he demanded every bit of patience that I could possibly muster because he wanted what he wanted when he wanted it. Now.

Some children come from seemingly caring and supportive homes. Others are raised in a culture of gangs and the whole assortment of violence associated with that lifestyle. Many more are raised around domestic violence, criminal activity, substance abuse and/or uninvolved parents.

It won't always make sense why a particular kid drives you crazy. But you have to be consistent in your enforcement of rules, and that can be tricky. What may be horrendous behavior for one child may be good behavior for another one.

Regardless of a child's background or any empathy you may have for him, safety issues should be addressed firmly and without hesitation. Disruptive behavior needs to be addressed quickly because it can and will agitate the others. Seemingly minor behavioral issues can quickly escalate. A fire begins with a flame.

What if a juvenile incarcerated for armed robbery throws his playing cards down on a table and hollers, *That's bullshit!* and walks away with a *Fuck you!* What if you know he has court in two days to determine if he will be prosecuted as an adult? What if you have a rapport with him and he responds to **your request** to speak with him **in his room**? As he's going there he's threatening to *kill you* and everyone you know, but he **does enter his room** without the use of physical force. He tells you to *Fuck off*; however, he *allows* you to **secure the steel door** to his room.

Safety has been maintained. Give him time to cool down. Later, based on your evaluation of him, further decisions can then be made regarding further consequences.

Regardless of their guilt, incarceration does suck. No pity: They did what they did. However, your understanding of and appreciation for their situation can be a driving force behind building a rapport or, at least, establishing some kind of mutual tolerance.

What are you bringing to each and every interaction? Rest assured, you are bringing something. We all do.

Why do you get along with some but not others? It's not always about them.

Logic versus Emotion

Guards will repeatedly hear these simple words, *Fuck you*. Those words will be yelled at you. They will be said to you with venom spitting. They may be said in passing, *Fuck you*. What do you do in response?

Certainly, it can be reasonably argued that saying *fuck you* to someone is disrespectful. However, I have said it and worse to my friends without meaning any disrespect.

They are just two words, *Fuck you*. Don't let them escalate into violence.

These are also *simple* words: *You're a bitch*; *you're an asshole; motherfucker; cunt;* and the ones that really piss me off, *You're* [a] *racist*.

Some people don't like you. It's simple: Some think you are an asshole, a bitch, a douchebag and the stupid list goes on. Sometimes though, their opinions can be spot on correct.

About a year ago, I had a kid, Gary, angrily tell me that I was wrong and being *fuckin' unfair* when I took a privilege away from him because he wasn't participating in a required activity. He even called me *a racist* before walking away. My immediate reaction was to give him a piece of my mind. Instead, I took a controlled breath, approached him (feeling quite irritated) and asked, *What's going on? You seem off.*

He told me that his parents never want him to return home. They wanted to *disown* him. I listened. Afterward, I spoke with Gary's clinician who confirmed everything. He was facing foster care. When I saw Gary later, I apologized for having been short with him earlier. And I also said, *I'm sorry for what you are going through.*

We are educated about the psychological and physical effects of abuse, neglect and trauma. We are educated about the gang culture. However, we can all-too-often forget that these detained juveniles are dealing with some profound life and family issues. If the opportunity presents itself, engage in a conversation and something important may be achieved: rapport.

At one time or another, most of us have inadvertently said something hurtful to someone. We have used words that we immediately regretted. In the *real world*, there's an opportunity to talk and try to apologize. But, incarceration is a highly structured environment where there are quick responses for certain statements made. I've heard guards complain about being micromanaged; I hate it. It makes me feel like I'm not trusted to do the job for which I have been hired. And yet, we expect incarcerated children to blindly accept being micromanaged.

Everything they say or do is constantly monitored and subject to a whole litany of repercussions. Like us, they will make mistakes. Unlike us, damn near every mistake made will be addressed with little regard for the circumstances behind the making of that mistake.

So, the next time a juvenile says something along the lines of a *fuck you*, evaluate the situation and explore the possibility of just talking with him about his inappropriate language without enforcing consequences. And if consequences are necessary, make them out of logic not emotion.

Always strive to react out of logic, not emotion.

Control

I hate staff who try to control me, not the situation.

The child and the situation are separate concepts. He has a history of experiences which form the foundation for how he responds to perceived threats. He may know that when grandpa raises his voice, someone is going to get *all-kinds-of-fucked-up*. It's a relatively simple association: When a man raises his voice, he remembers grandpa and prepares for broken bones and chaos.

Like war veterans, children exposed to trauma can suffer from PTSD. Post-Traumatic Stress Disorder is a psychiatric disorder that can occur following the experience or witnessing of a physically threatening event such as military combat, natural disaster, a serious accident or physical and sexual abuse.[7]

---

[7] American Psychiatric Association.

React to the situation, not to the individual.

In our facility when the juveniles are being walked through the corridors, they must hold their hands behind their backs. They often need reminders. Maybe someone is scratching his nose. Someone may wave to his case manager who waved to him. It's quite effective to merely say to the entire group, *Hands behind your back, please.* It's a courteous reminder that doesn't single anyone out. More often than not, that child will reposition his hands with an apology.

Failure to keep your hands behind your back can lead to a privilege loss. Nothing major but a loss which can then further agitate an already frustrated child. Is there any real benefit to enforcing a consequence when a courteous reminder can give him an opportunity to comply with the facility rules? If he does, facility rules have been enforced. Safety maintained. Everyone moves on.

We have the inherent power to enforce any decision we deem appropriate at the time and having the power to use force is no small consideration. If a rule violation is not threatening safety, avoid unnecessarily shaking that *hive*. Address issues quietly but firmly; a simple or subtle reminder may be all that is needed, *Please stop*. If he does, move on.

Control over power.

Sharif

Sharif was a reasonably talented, seventeen-year-old writer and quite insightful. He often showed me his latest pieces; I found some to be rather intriguing, well-constructed and deserving feedback.

He asked to be called Sharif in honor of his dead uncle who was reportedly killed in prison.

Sharif had been incarcerated numerous times for an assortment of violent crimes. We never talked about them; they weren't relevant to me. We had many conversations over the year we *knew* each other. More often than not they were brief, but I listened. And as it turned out, he listened too. Over time, I learned about Sharif's life. He learned about mine. Both in a sanitized but seemingly genuine way.

One day, while in the main corridor of our facility, he and I had a brief exchange. He asked if I could take him to the library. I told him that I would try, when things weren't so hectic. He remarked that I was just *an old, lazy man*. I responded that for someone wanting something from me, he was sorely lacking in social skills.

You know, for an old pathetic man, you're alright.

We fist bumped and parted ways.

Later, I did in fact take him to the library, and we discussed the presidential race, Trump-vs-Clinton. We agreed that the political landscape was rather bleak at best. He picked up Ray Bradbury's *Fahrenheit 451* and asked if I knew the book. I told him it had been decades since I had read it, but I remembered enough to recommend that he read it.

We over time talked about the struggles of the human race: wars over religion, territory and political ideologies; racism; and people getting overly *freaked out* about sexual orientation.

One day, Sharif was angry and in crisis. He was pissed off because court had not gone his way. He was facing more time (a substantial amount), and his mother wasn't coming to visitation as she usually did.

As I entered his pod which was housing eleven other detainees, he approached me quickly with clenched fists. I put my hands up and bladed away from him.

Sharif paused.

I said rather forcefully but quietly, *Whoa, what the fuck Shariff? Gimme me space. Talk to me. This ain't no joke. Fuckin' talk to me.*

That pause, filled with adrenaline and uncertainty, turned into a conversation **in his room**. His aggressive behavior was agitating the pod. Some were encouraging him. Our conversation only happened, when it did, after **he went to his room** as **instructed**. My first responsibility has to be to the group. That moment had been fraught with the potential for violence, but we met somewhere between it and calculated vulnerability.

That entire incident lasted no more than fifteen seconds, more likely ten.

Days after the fact, I told him that I was proud of him, *I really thought you were going to hit me.*

I asked him, *What the hell stopped you? You were pissed.*

Sharif didn't say much in response. But, I understood.

Maternal Instincts

Doris Statler

The one thing I believe we all need, crave and want is a sense of love and belonging. It's hard for me to comprehend how other children have been raised or fully grasp the situations they have been exposed to.

Every child is different. Some you like; some you don't; and others grow on you because they remind you of your own kids. Maybe, they have criminal charges your own child could have once stumbled across. Call it luck.

For some kids, detention can be a revolving door and you get a headache just by hearing their names. We try not to talk about them because, if we do, they will surely show up within the week.

We had one boy come to our facility several times for minor offenses. The last time he was detained, he had been with some kid who was shooting at a house with a BB gun. The owner came out with a real gun while on his phone with 911. The kid with the BB gun ran. Bobby could not run. He was more than a little overweight and had a prosthetic leg.

Bobby's mother called us every day to check on him. She was at least concerned about her son, unlike many parents. Nonetheless, she aggravated us to death.

Bobby kept hiding a 5x7 photo of him and his mother under his mattress. Photos are considered contraband in their cells. We kept removing his photo during the cell searches and returning it to his personal folder on the pod. Almost every morning we'd go into his room and find the picture under his mattress. I couldn't get upset with him because it was his connection to home.

He and I had a bond of sorts. I think some of it was because I reminded him of his mom.

After he was released, his mother called and asked for me. When I got on the phone, I could hear Bobby crying in the background. She said he was *hysterical* because he was afraid he'd be locked up again. Apparently, some of his friends had done something illegal and were telling the police he was with them. I told her to put Bobby on the phone. I got him to stop crying. He told me his version of what had happened, and I told him to tell the police the truth.

Weeks later she called asking for my address; Bobby wanted to send me an invitation to his High School graduation. I never received it. Although I know I couldn't have gone, it meant a lot that he wanted me to be a part of his big moment.

To this day, I often wonder how he is doing?

Family

As soon as one problem resident leaves, he will be replaced with at least one more. It's a never-ending cycle of intakes-fights-releases. Not every juvenile we encounter will be aggressive or even a problem, but the majority of them don't come to visit because they were just in the *wrong place at the wrong time*. Most of them are locked up because of things they did and some of those things were violent felony acts during which innocent people were victimized.

Kids join gangs because they want to have a sense of belonging, a sense of *family*. Being detained fosters a similar need for belonging. A lot of them don't have a functional family or at least a family that they can count on. Even if they do, they are now separated from them. So, when they are detained, they look for safety. Enough of the population is locked up long enough to become part of something bigger; that something doesn't include the guards. The longer they are locked up, the more they feel mistreated by *the system*; and in their detention culture, the guards are that system.

> *We're grown ass men.*
> *This is bullshit.*
> *You fuckin' cop wannabes.*

Despite the verbal abuses and inevitable altercations, you will be required to continue with your duties. When you feed them dinner, you may hear someone yelling, *Fuck you, asshole. Wait till I get out of this room, I'm gonna to kill you.* The one threatening you may be the one who recently shared with you that his family *sucks meth dick* and that he *hates his fuckin' whore of a mother.* You listened and empathized, like a parent listening to his own child. He even shed a tear. Now, he's just cussing you like a dog.

It's a dysfunctional family, but there is a family dynamic.

We are trained to not judge a child for his crimes because all children should be treated with respect. And yet we (as guards) can often forget to respect each other. I'm guilty of it. I have reviewed videos of incidents and exclaimed, *Oh, to hell with that! What the hell was he thinking? What an idiot.* Well, guess what? Children have gone off on me despite all my best efforts. It's easy to sit back, not having been involved in an incident, and nitpick the hell out of it, be in judgment of it; but I too have made poor decisions during moments of crisis.

Reports, words on a page, can't capture the emotional dynamics between you and the detainee. Video, likewise, sanitizes everything. Your actions will be reviewed and judged based on those reports and video. Your perceived conduct during a crisis isolates weeks, maybe months, of interactions to a few chaotic moments.

While detainees may be verbally and physically aggressive toward us, we have to continue treating them with respect, while doing no harm - while avoiding certain career ending mistakes.

We have known guards who were terminated because they had crossed some line from a person reacting to violence to being deemed violent and/or abusive. More than a handful of them were wonderful with the population to whom they had dedicated their lives. In the briefest of moments, they were gone.

It's hard for a guard not to feel like everyone is against him, to feel like that *black sheep*.

Mahiri's Two Cents
Chacha Mahiri

Often, given the challenging and unpredictable nature of working with court-involved-youth, it's easy to forget that behind their ice-cold stares, don't-fuck-with-me personas and violent tendencies, they are children.

We work with kids from diverse upbringings; some are born into the criminal life and glorify it. Some have taken a *prank too far* or were at the *wrong place at the wrong time*. Regardless, once they wind up in the system, we have to dissociate our personal beliefs from our job in order to provide a safe, structured and *nurturing* environment.

I grew up in the cultural belly of East Africa before migrating to the U.S. in 2001. While I had my rebellious and teenage angst years, I didn't take anything for granted. I saw the machinations of an unrelenting justice that took no prisoners in my native country. Vigilante justice was the norm. I saw kids set ablaze with gasoline for petty crimes: snatching a woman's purse, stealing fruit, vandalism. Corruption was rampant.

I believe that my cross-cultural experience has allowed me to establish important links with these children. They build their trust and respect for you, or lack of, based on how you treat them. Setting boundaries and expectations can help a day run smoothly and alleviate unforeseen conflicts. Sometimes kids will just be kids and, no matter what you do, more intrusive measures may be needed in critical situations.

The simple act of listening can often be a more effective solution than scolding or taking a kid's privilege as punishment.

I've had kids haul insults and profanities incessantly at me and yet remained patient and understanding. While their behavior is not acceptable, I know their anger might be stemming from something far removed from me.

Some of our kids are extremely smart and superb manipulators, almost chameleon like. They'll spend their time studying you; learning what makes you tick; dissecting your mannerisms to the minutest of detail. A few will bide their time, waiting for that opportunity to strike, to hurt you.

Jay understands our facility rules and policies pretty well. He'll tell everyone, *I've been locked up since I was twelve. I know how to work the system.* Jay finesses staff to get what he wants. A new kid joined the unit, and Jay told him, *I run shit here. You better put some respect on it.* What started as small slights and comments quickly turned into Jay loud-mouthing my fellow new guard. My attempts to redirect his behavior were met with belligerent, verbal abuses. I was blindsided by how far Jay was willing to go in order to *demonstrate* his power on the unit. Jay erupted from his chair while unleashing a tirade of eccentric, racial epithets at me. More stringent measures had to be taken to address his threatening behavior.

The following day I still had to work with Jay. I couldn't hold any grudges or let that racially charged event cloud my judgment. I still had to treat him fairly while holding him responsible for his actions, as I would any other resident on the unit.

While I see myself as a role model, hoping to impact Jay to turn his life around, I can only hope to be an agent that precipitates a spark. After all, Jay is seventeen-years-old and imminently waiting to be tried for his delinquent behavior. Only he can light that match for the life ahead of him.

Final Report:

I was attacked by Jorge which really pissed me off.

He was locked down earlier for assaulting another kid, Ramon, which had also pissed me off because he hurt Ramon badly. Jorge requested toothpaste. I looked through his door window. He appeared calm. Although he had a substantial history of assaulting guards and other children, I saw nothing in his behavior alerting me to anything being amiss. I had him sit on his bunk with his hands behind his back. As I opened his door, he charged out, headbutted me and bit my chest.

Later that night, while licking my wounds and mending my pride, I started the process of mentally preparing for my next shift. Somehow, I would have to drag my ass to work and conduct myself as a professional.

The following day (while patrolling the pods) I said, *Good morning,* to Jorge when I saw him. He wanted nothing of it - unlike Jay, Bobby, Sharif, Gary, Ramon, David, Jennifer and a few others who responded with their pleasantries when I greeted them.

It was a new day and even if my words were self-serving and utilitarian, I genuinely meant them on some primitive level:

Good morning...